**JOIN THE JACK DALY HYPER SALES GROWTH MEMBERSHIP PROGRAM, AND LEARN ALL THE SECRETS TO EXPONENTIAL GROWTH.**

In Jack's thirty years in the Sales Training Space, sales managers, salespeople, and corporate executives have asked Jack to develop this Sales Training Program.

Here's what you'll get:

- Monthly Conference Calls with Jack and Team
- Peer-to-Peer Networking & Learning
- Structured Accountability
- Jack Daly University Core Curriculum Content
- Interactive Group Email List

**To join, visit www.jackdalytraining.com/secret**

# Sales Success AHAs

## 140 AHAs to Grow Your Sales

## Jack Daly and Jeff Shavitz

**THiNK**aha®

### An Actionable Business Journal

E-mail: info@thinkaha.com
20660 Stevens Creek Blvd., Suite 210
Cupertino, CA 95014

⇨ Please go to http://aha.pub/SalesSuccessAHAs to read this AHAbook and to share the individual AHAmessages that resonate with you.

Published by THiNKaha®
20660 Stevens Creek Blvd., Suite 210, Cupertino, CA 95014
http://thinkaha.com
E-mail: info@thinkaha.com

First Printing: May 2017
Paperback ISBN: 978-1-61699-193-7   1-61699-193-3
eBook ISBN: 978-1-61699-192-0   1-61699-192-5
Place of Publication: Silicon Valley, California, USA
Paperback Library of Congress Number: 2016940825

# Dedication

Dedicated to all the sales managers and salespeople. Without their positions, businesses would have few to no sales. Sales is a real skill, just like any other business discipline, so congratulations on your thirst to better yourself in your profession.

## Acknowledgement

Both Jack and Jeff wish to acknowledge Young Presidents' Organization (YPO). Because of this group, we had the opportunity to meet each other, develop a personal friendship, and collaborate on writing this book together. It's been a fun journey and all the better that we both have a new golf buddy!

# How to Read a THiNKaha® Book
## A Note from the Publisher

The THiNKaha series is the CliffsNotes of the 21st century. The value of these books is that they are contextual in nature. Although the actual words won't change, their meaning will change every time you read one as your context will change. Experience your own "AHA!" moments ("AHAmessages™") with a THiNKaha book; AHAmessages are looked at as "actionable" moments—think of a specific project you're working on, an event, a sales deal, a personal issue, etc. and see how the AHAmessages in this book can inspire your own AHAmessages, something that you can specifically act on. Here's how to read one of these books and have it work for you:

1. Read a THiNKaha book (these slim and handy books should only take about 15–20 minutes of your time!) and write down one to three actionable items you thought of while reading it. Each journal-style THiNKaha book is equipped with space for you to write down your notes and thoughts underneath each AHAmessage.

2. Mark your calendar to re-read this book again in 30 days.

3. Repeat step #1 and write down one to three more AHAmessages that grab you this time. I guarantee that they will be different than the first time. BTW: this is also a great time to reflect on the actions taken from the last set of AHAmessages you wrote down.

After reading a THiNKaha book, writing down your AHAmessages, re-reading it, and writing down more AHAmessages, you'll begin to see how these books contextually apply to you. THiNKaha books advocate for continuous, lifelong learning. They will help you transform your AHAs into actionable items with tangible results until you no longer have to say "AHA!" to these moments—they'll become part of your daily practice as you continue to grow and learn.

As The AHA Guy at THiNKaha, I definitely practice what I preach. I read 2-3 AHAbooks a month in addition to those that we publish and take away two to three different action items from each of them every time. Please e-mail me your AHAs today!

Mitchell Levy
publisher@thinkaha.com

**THiNK**aha®

# Contents

# Introduction

### Jeff's Thoughts about Jack

*"Learn from the best. I have been very fortunate to have developed a unique friendship with Jack; without sounding patronizing, the man is truly remarkable on so many levels. He just gets it and says it how it is. Even when using an F-Bomb to highlight something of utmost importance, his delivery is powerful, his comments thought provoking, and he is just a great guy and I'm happy to call him my friend."*

### Jack's Thoughts about Jeff

*"I meet tens of thousands of people per year. I travel over 300 days per year. I barely can remember a person one hour after meeting them because of my hectic schedule. Jeff stood out. We immediately created a friendship. Although I'm almost 20 years his senior, I've learned so much from him. I love his energy and his perspective on business and life. Can't wait to do book two together. BAM!"*

# Section I

## The Sales Manager's Inner Thoughts
## – by Jack Daly

The sales manager is a critical position in any organization. Are you the cheerleader or the coach? Do you act as the parent? When do you criticize? When do you motivate? It's a tough job, and once you earn the respect of your team, magic happens. Sales start rolling in, and revenue and profitability grow. Learn the thoughts and actions of a great sales manager.

# 1

A sales manager's job is not to grow sales.
A sales manager's job is to grow people —
in quantity and quality. @IronManJack

_____

_____

_____

# 2

Implement consistent recognition systems
to acknowledge great salesmanship.
@IronManJack

_____

_____

_____

# 3

Recruiting is a pro-active process, not a responsive solution. @IronManJack

_____

_____

_____

# 4

Be an enthusiastic leader — you are the message. @IronManJack

_____

_____

_____

# 5

Minimum standards of performance should be negotiated with each individual associate. @IronManJack

_____

_____

_____

# 6

Orchestrate at least monthly sales meetings, addressing improvement of sales skills.
@IronManJack

_____

_____

_____

# 7

Have each salesperson establish and carry a "target list" of where their business will come from in the next 12 months.
@IronManJack

_____

_____

_____

# 8

Avoid making decisions your
employees can make. @IronManJack

_____

_____

_____

# 9

Some executives create more enthusiasm
when they leave a room than when they
enter it. Which are you? @IronManJack

_____

_____

_____

# 10

Recruiting is a process, not an event.
It must be ongoing and continuous.
@IronManJack

_____

_____

_____

# 11

Customization is the future. Give each customer what they want, the way they want it. @IronManJack

_____

_____

_____

# 12

No statue was ever erected to the memory of a person who thought it best to leave well enough alone. @IronManJack

_____

_____

_____

# 13

The secret to successfully managing people is to understand what they really want out of their careers — then give it to them. @IronManJack

_____

_____

_____

# 14

Go after the 80% on each initiative and forget the remaining 20% — it's rarely worth the extra effort. @IronManJack

_____

_____

_____

# 15

Don't hire only people who look and act like you. A mix will create a more effective team.
@IronManJack

_____

_____

_____

# 16

People are different — lead accordingly.
@IronManJack

_____

_____

_____


# 17

People love applause — offer it generously.
@IronManJack

_____

_____

_____

# 18

Start every sales meeting with a standing ovation. Prioritize recognition.
@IronManJack

_____

_____

_____

# 19

Every leader should do progress reviews (not formal annual performance reviews) with their associates at least every quarter.
@IronManJack

_____

_____

_____

# 20

Every leader should have a recruiting target list, identified from one's networking efforts. @IronManJack

_____

_____

_____

# 21

As soon as the decision to hire has been
made and the employment offer accepted,
order business cards that day!
@IronManJack

_____

_____

_____

# 22

Compensation reviews are for past performance; progress reviews are for future commitment. @IronManJack

---

---

---

# 23

Are you a technician or a cheerleader? @IronManJack

---

---

---

# 24

The best job for an employee who constantly says, "Because that's the way we've always done it," is with one of your competitors. @IronManJack

_____

_____

_____

# 25

You generally need to change only one thing to turn an average performer into a top performer: their attitude. @IronManJack

_____

_____

_____

# 26

If you hire mediocre sales folks, the top producers lose their challenge. If you hire top people, you create healthy competition. @IronManJack

_____

_____

_____

# 27

Most people fail not because of technical knowledge but because of attitude or people skills problems. @IronManJack

_____

_____

_____

# 28

One mistake will never kill you. The same mistake over and over will. @IronManJack

_____

_____

_____

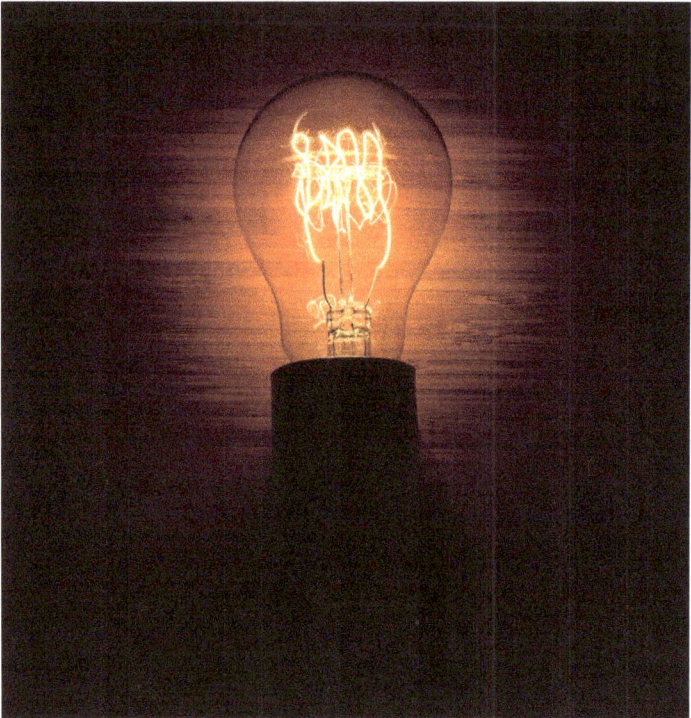

# Section II

## The Salesperson's Inner Thoughts
### – by Jeff Shavitz

It's hard getting up every morning and selling, but that's my job. Being a sales manager is so easy. It's just managing, not selling. Maybe I'll choose that job. Nah, I love being a salesperson. It's who I am, it's what I do. Learn my secrets to being a great and highly paid salesperson.

# 29

A sales manager and a salesperson are very different jobs. Most people are not great at both. Which are you? @JeffShavitz

_____

_____

_____

# 30

Do you like selling a product or a service — or does it really matter? Selling is selling. @JeffShavitz

_____

_____

_____

# 31

When you graduated college, did you think
about sales as your profession?
I didn't but I wish I had. @JeffShavitz

_____

_____

_____

# 32

What are you good at? Opening
relationships, developing relationships,
closing deals — all important traits.
Know yourself. @JeffShavitz

_____

_____

_____

# 33

Try to find a residual-based product or service — recurring revenue is a beautiful thing for a salesperson. @JeffShavitz

_____

_____

_____

# 34

Being a sales professional is a real profession. Take it seriously and become a master salesperson. @JeffShavitz

_____

_____

_____

# 35

Would you suggest to your son/daughter/ grandchild to pursue a career in sales? @JeffShavitz

_____

_____

_____

# 36

It would be nice to once be acknowledged for my hard work. @JeffShavitz

_____

_____

_____

# 37

I'm great at selling and horrible at doing the administrative work. I wish my sales manager would assign me a person.
@JeffShavitz

_____

_____

_____

# 38

Great selling characteristics is similar to the person who plays great defense in sports. You just need to try really hard.
@JeffShavitz

_____

_____

_____

# 39

Working from home takes real discipline. Too easy to watch soap operas, Ellen, and Oprah reruns. @JeffShavitz

_____

_____

_____

# 40

Our sales manager always mentions the 80/20 rule — I need to figure out if it's really 90/10 or 70/30 with my clients. @JeffShavitz

_____

_____

_____

# 41

Does your sales manager believe in a T&E budget for you to take clients golfing and out for dinner throughout the year? @JeffShavitz

_____

_____

_____

# 42

You should know within a few days
if your new hire is going to make it.
If not, fire quickly. @JeffShavitz

_____

_____

_____

# 43

I can't stand all the paperwork I need to fill out on a daily basis for my sales manager. I just want to sell. @JeffShavitz

---

---

---

# 44

Write down your annual goals on paper before your sales manager requests them in an Excel spreadsheet. @JeffShavitz

_____

_____

_____

# 45

It's all about closing the deal. At some point, it's "Put Up or Shut Up." @JeffShavitz

_____

_____

_____

# 46

A day can be very long without a sale.
So get a sale to celebrate. @JeffShavitz

_____

_____

_____

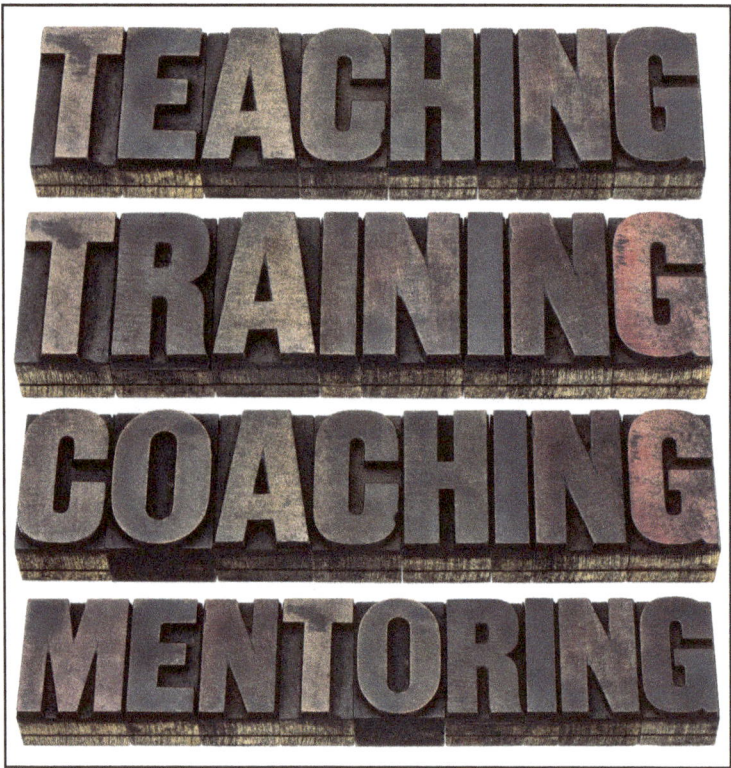

# Section III

## How to Mentor Your Team to Realize Optimal Results – by Jack Daly

Teamwork: without the parent/child respectful relationship, the sales manager/salesperson relationship doesn't work, and the company will not have its projected sales. Sales managers have a unique skillset that when mastered, creates a company vision and morale that is quite special, whether for a small business or a corporate bureaucracy.

# 47

Once you have decided on your mission, go for it as if your life depended on it. @IronManJack

_____

_____

_____

# 48

You must teach, counsel, or motivate
someone every day. @IronManJack

_____

_____

_____

# 49

You can achieve more with a "we will" attitude as a leader-manager than a "you will" attitude. @IronManJack

_____

_____

_____

# 50

The manager's most expensive time is the time between when you truly lose faith in someone and when you do something about it. @IronManJack

_____

_____

_____

# 51

The best way to avoid problems is not to hire them. @IronManJack

_____

_____

_____

# 52

A good sales strategy is to grow your businesses with the customers you already have. @IronManJack

_____

_____

_____

# 53

Praise loudly and criticize quietly. @IronManJack

_____

_____

_____

# 54

In the race for success, the speed of the leader determines the pace of the pack.
@IronManJack

---

---

---

# 55

The best ideas for improving a job come from those who do it every day.
@IronManJack

_____

_____

_____

# 56

Authentic feedback flows in all directions.
@IronManJack

_____

_____

_____

# 57

The window to the future gives better guidance than the mirror. Focus on actions with your associates going forward. @IronManJack

_____

_____

_____

# 58

When people you respect recommend books, read them. @IronManJack

_____

_____

_____

# 59

You can buy a person's time and talent —
but loyalty and enthusiasm must be earned.
@IronManJack

_____

_____

_____

# 60

Business is a game of intensity and
emotion. Deliver both. @IronManJack

_____

_____

_____

# 61

Recruiting is the never-ending process
of looking for qualified candidates for
employment. @IronManJack

_____

_____

_____

# 62

Positive reinforcement of those things people do right will do more to create a success environment than "constructive criticism." @IronManJack

_____

_____

_____

# 63

You don't have to be perfect, just better than the competition. @IronManJack

_____

_____

_____

# 64

Don't tell employees how to do the job. Tell them what needs to be done. @IronManJack

_____

_____

_____

# 65

What the leader says is important;
what the leader does is critical.
@IronManJack

_____

_____

_____

# 66

Just as athletes are attracted to winning teams, so it is with employees in business.
@IronManJack

---

---

---

# 67

Help each new hire to be successful early after they join you. Assign a peer as a buddy for 60 days. @IronManJack

_____

_____

_____

# 68

Office image and work commitment created in the 1st month, 1st day, and 1st hour is difficult to change. Make it a positive one. @IronManJack

_____

_____

_____

# 69

The mediocre teacher tells.
The good teacher explains.
The superior teacher demonstrates.
The great teacher inspires.
@IronManJack

_____

_____

_____

# 70

Learn the difference between running
a meeting and leading a group.
@IronManJack

_____

_____

_____

# 71

Highly recommend reading
"Networking — Get Connected"
by Jeff Shavitz. @IronManJack

_____

_____

_____

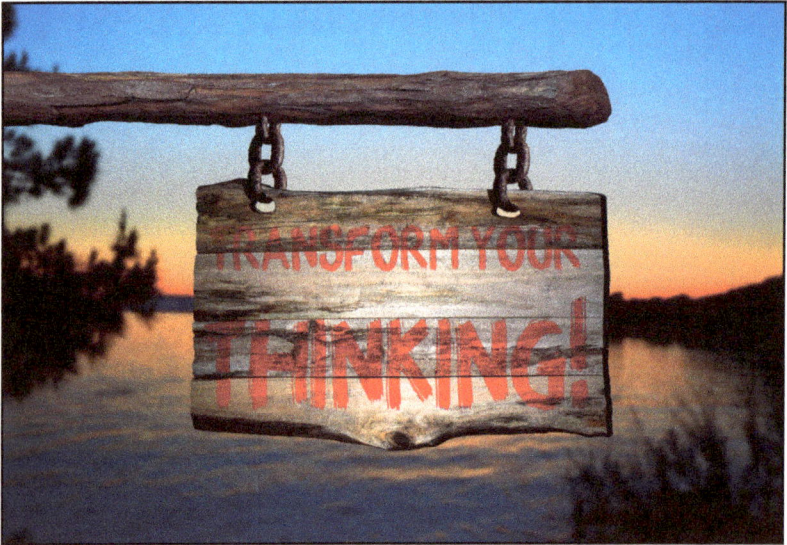

# Section IV

## The Proper Mindset of the Salesperson – by Jeff Shavitz

Salespeople deserve to make lots of money—
when they are great at their craft. It's hard work,
and any salesperson who has the courage to
work on commission, I commend you. Learn the
psychology of the successful salesperson and
watch your business grow!

# 72

Sales, sales, sales are critical words in the selling business, like location, location, location in the real estate business. @JeffShavitz

_____

_____

_____

# 73

Don't forget to write a thank you note (or an email will do) to your new customer to acknowledge the business. @JeffShavitz

_____

_____

_____

# 74

Do you know who your customers are —
I mean, do you really know?
Only you know the answer. @JeffShavitz

_____

_____

_____

# 75

Read "Size Doesn't Matter — Why Small Business Is BIG Business." I loved the book; oh yeah, I wrote it! @JeffShavitz

_____

_____

_____

# 76

A sales meeting with a prospect can take 1/2 a day by the time you drive, prepare & have the meeting. Use your time wisely. @JeffShavitz

_____

_____

_____

# 77

Know when to be quiet and just listen.
It's harder to do than you think.
Shut up! @JeffShavitz

_____

_____

_____

# 78

Get your sales manager out of the office to develop an authentic relationship with them: lunch, cocktails, weekend. @JeffShavitz

---

---

---

# 79

Find a role model and then learn from the best. @JeffShavitz

---

---

---

# 80

When was the last time you attended a sales conference or read a sales book on how to improve your skills? It's never too late.
@JeffShavitz

_____

_____

_____

# 81

Amazing that my sales manager can't create an incentive plan that excites me and is great for the company at the same time. @JeffShavitz

_____

_____

_____

# 82

Do you believe in the product or service you are selling? If you don't, find a new company. @JeffShavitz

_____

_____

_____

# 83

Making money is hard. Be proud of yourself when you earn that big commission check. @JeffShavitz

_____

_____

_____

# 84

Selling is hard — you shouldn't forget that, nor should your sales manager. @JeffShavitz

_____

_____

_____

# 85

I loved reading "Small Business Aha Messages" by Jeff Shavitz. I wonder why. @JeffShavitz

_____

_____

_____

# 86

Jack Daly is the greatest sales trainer I've ever heard — which is why I asked him to co-author a book with me. @JeffShavitz

_____

_____

_____

# 87

Get organized the night before to have a productive following day. @JeffShavitz

_____

_____

_____

# 88

Working just a few hours each weekend will make a huge difference in your annual performance. @JeffShavitz

_____

_____

_____

# 89

If you're feeling comfortable with your sales
production, start feeling uncomfortable.
@JeffShavitz

_____

_____

_____

# 90

Meet with the pres. of your company to truly
understand the vision he/she has for the
business. It will help you sell better.
@JeffShavitz

_____

_____

_____

# 91

Don't forget to ask family and friends for potential contacts. @JeffShavitz

_____

_____

_____

# 92

When in the sales zone, don't check email
or text messages or become distracted.
Sell, sell, sell. @JeffShavitz

_____

_____

_____

# 93

Have your sales manager pay for you to
attend a Jack Daly sales training seminar.
Best use of your time and money.
@JeffShavitz

_____

_____

_____

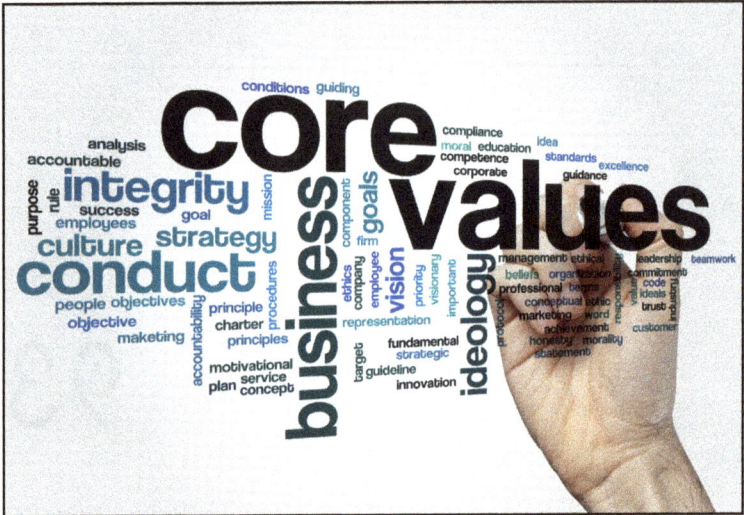

# Section V

## It's All about the Culture
## – by Jack Daly

What really differentiates most companies when there are so many similar products and services in the marketplace is the CULTURE! Yes, the culture of an organization is that special "thing" that will take a company to a higher level of success.

# 94

To use a mission statement effectively, you must Enroll, Empower, and Recognize. @IronManJack

_____

_____

_____

# 95

A successful sales culture understands the value that "relationships developed" vs "transactions completed" is more important.
@IronManJack

_____

_____

_____

# 96

Everyone in the first 30 days wonders if they made a mistake in joining your company. Communicate regularly to overcome this. @IronManJack

_____

_____

_____

# 97

Without a leader committed to learning, an organization will never approach its potential for success. @IronManJack

_____

_____

_____

# 98

Identify new role models and mentors.
Align the new with the experienced.
@IronManJack

\_\_\_\_\_

\_\_\_\_\_

\_\_\_\_\_

# 99

Remember, I don't care how much you
know until I know how much you care.
@IronManJack

\_\_\_\_\_

\_\_\_\_\_

\_\_\_\_\_

# 100

Implementation is bottom-up; commitment and support are top-down. @IronManJack

_____

_____

_____

# 101

Change is inevitable; growth is optional.
@IronManJack

_____

_____

_____

# 102

If no one is ever at work at 6:00AM or 8:00PM, your company is in trouble. @IronManJack

_____

_____

_____

# 103

It's not the people you fire who make your life miserable; it's the people you don't fire who make your life miserable. @IronManJack

_____

_____

_____

# 104

Caring is contagious; spread it around.
@IronManJack

_____

_____

_____

# 105

Knowledgeable companies communicate.
@IronManJack

_____

_____

_____


# 106

Early established habits are difficult to change — make them positive ones.
@IronManJack

_____

_____

_____

# 107

Good interview thought: Would I want to have dinner with this person outside of the interview forum? @IronManJack

_____

_____

_____

# 108

Another interview thought: Would I look forward to sitting side by side with them on a coast-to-coast flight? @IronManJack

_____

_____

_____

# 109

Your salespeople should be optimistic, energetic cheerleaders. If they're not, changes are necessary (not necessarily w/ them). @IronManJack

_____

_____

_____

# 110

You cannot motivate other people, but you can put them in an environment where they will motivate themselves. @IronManJack

_____

_____

_____

# 111

If your goal is satisfied clients, your goal is far too modest. @IronManJack

_____

_____

_____

# 112

Never start someone until you have the personal time to commit to an effective orientation/welcome. @IronManJack

_____

_____

_____

# 113

Implement a first-day celebration for all new hires. Make it an event! @IronManJack

_____

_____

_____

# 114

People are down on what they are not up on — communicate. @IronManJack

_____

_____

_____

# 115

There is no limit to what a person can do or where that person can go if they don't mind who gets the credit. @IronManJack

_____

_____

_____

# 116

If you recruit people who are smarter than you are, you prove that you are smarter than they are. @IronManJack

_____

_____

_____

# 117

In a world of change, you either make history or you are history. @IronManJack

_____

_____

_____

# Section VI

## Are You Selling a Product, Service—or Yourself? - by Jeff Shavitz

The market is competitive. The laws of supply and demand determine the market price. How can you differentiate your product from the competition when so many products and services are similar? YOU are the difference. Sell yourself in conjunction with your company's vision and watch your revenues soar.

# 118

It all starts with that one sale.
Don't ever forget that. @JeffShavitz

_____

_____

_____

# 119

Do you respect your sales manager?
Do they make you a better salesperson
and more importantly, a better person?
@JeffShavitz

_____

_____

_____

# 120

Think about what you would do differently
if you held the position of sales manager in
your company. Then do those things.
@JeffShavitz

_____

_____

_____

# 121

Are you selling your company's brand, your product, yourself — or all 3 at the same time? @JeffShavitz

_____

_____

_____

# 122

Help your other sales associates. We're all competitive, but what comes around goes around. @JeffShavitz

_____

_____

_____

# 123

Don't steal a client from your fellow salesperson. You're being short-sighted on how to build your career. @JeffShavitz

_____

_____

_____

# 124

Speaking of residual income, read "The Power of Residual Income — You Can Bank on It" to learn types of residual companies. @JeffShavitz

_____

_____

_____

# 125

When was the last time your sales manager
had a 1x1 meeting with you to share
thoughts on how you can grow in
the position? @JeffShavitz

_____

_____

_____

# 126

Commissioned salespeople deserve to
make a ton of money. Maybe even more
than the president of the company.
What do you think? @JeffShavitz

_____

_____

_____

# 127

Aren't you always selling in some capacity?
I think so. @JeffShavitz

_____

_____

_____

# 128

Trying to land this sale has now become a game for me. It's no longer about the money. I'm going to win over this prospect.
@JeffShavitz

_____

_____

_____

# 129

What is my upward mobility in this company? I'm just a salesperson. The sky is the limit. @JeffShavitz

_____

_____

_____

# 130

We all know the sales manager has a "cushy" job. I just wish the president knew who really did all the selling around here. @JeffShavitz

_____

_____

_____

# 131

Telemarketing is a type of selling. Creating a relationship over the phone is hard to do; if you can, you have a sales gift.

@JeffShavitz

_____

_____

_____

# 132

Are you born as a salesperson, or can you learn to be a salesperson? I'm curious to hear what you think. @JeffShavitz

_____

_____

_____

# 133

Have you ever received a cold call during dinner and tried to hire that salesperson for your company b/c he sounded so good? @JeffShavitz

_____

_____

_____

# 134

Why are the same people always on the
President's Sales Trip? I am going to
work hard the next 12 months, as
I want to be on it. @JeffShavitz

_____

_____

_____

# 135

Customers would rather buy a good product from an extraordinary salesperson than a great product from a horrible salesperson. @JeffShavitz

_____

_____

_____

# 136

Salespeople look to their sales manager as their coach and confidant to help them solve problems. @JeffShavitz

_____

_____

_____

# 137

Systems are a critical way to manage your people. Get a great CRM. @JeffShavitz

_____

_____

_____

# 138

It's all about the people. Keep the great ones and let go of the bad performers. @JeffShavitz

_____

_____

_____

# 139

There is a fine line between being friends with your sales team. Walk the line carefully. @JeffShavitz

_____

_____

_____

# 140

Look in the mirror: Are you really working
as hard as you can? Don't fool yourself.
@JeffShavitz

_____

_____

_____

# About the Authors

**Jack Daly** is a professional sales coach, speaker, and expert in corporate culture, inspiring audiences to take action in customer loyalty and personal motivation. Jack's biography is a testament as to how he delivers explosive sales keynotes, sales workshops, and corporate culture workshops.

Jack brings over thirty years of field-proven experience from a starting base with CPA firm Arthur Andersen to the CEO level of several national companies. Jack is a proven CEO/Entrepreneur, having built six companies into national firms, two of which he subsequently sold to the Wall Street firms of Solomon Brothers and First Boston.

In 1985, Jack relocated to California from the East Coast and started a mortgage company with three colleagues. As CEO, Jack led the company through robust growth in its initial eighteen months to 750 employees and twenty-two offices nationwide, producing $350 million per month in mortgages. In its first three years, the company reported profits of $42 million.

In 1998, working as a senior partner in a five-year-old privately held enterprise, Jack helped the company be recognized as Entrepreneur of the Year by Ernst & Young and ranked #10 on the Inc. 5000 List of the Fastest Growing Firms Nationwide.

He holds a bachelor's degree in accounting, a master's degree in business administration, and was a Captain in the US Army.

Jack Daly is an accomplished author of books, audio, and DVD programs. To learn more or subscribe to his free email newsletter, visit www.jackdaly.net.

**Jeff Shavitz** is a successful entrepreneur whose passion and purpose for creating "his life" was the driving force behind leaving his lucrative position with Lehman Brothers to enter the world of entrepreneurship.

Jeff co-founded Charge Card Systems, Inc. (CCS), a national credit card processing company that helped merchants with their processing requirements, including the acceptance of Visa, MasterCard, American Express, and Discover. The company grew to more than 700 sales agents throughout the country, with three regional offices. In 2012, Jeff and his partners sold the business to Card Connect, owned by private equity firm FTV Capital.

After successfully selling CCS, Jeff's passion was working with small to mid-sized companies, which was the foundation of launching TrafficJamming LLC, a virtual membership group comprised of different business services for independent business owners and entrepreneurs to help grow their companies.

Author of four other books, including number-one Amazon bestseller *Size Doesn't Matter—Why Small Business Is BIG Business*, Jeff actively participates in business, civic, and philanthropic organizations, including the Young Presidents' Organization.

He graduated from Tufts University and spent one semester at the London School of Economics. He is married with three children, and besides family, health, and world peace, his selfish goal is to play the 100 top golf courses in the world! To learn more about Jeff and his business, visit www.trafficjamming.com.

# AHAthat™

AHAthat makes it easy to share, author, and promote content. There are over 37,000 quotes (AHAmessages™) by thought leaders from around the world that you can share in seconds for free.

For those who want to author their own book, we have time-tested proven processes that allow you to write your AHAbook™ of 140 digestible, bite-sized morsels in eight hours or less. Once your content is on AHAthat, you have a customized link that you can use to have your fans/advocates share your content and help grow your network.

➲ Start sharing: **http://AHAthat.com**

➲ Start authoring: **http://AHAthat.com/Author**

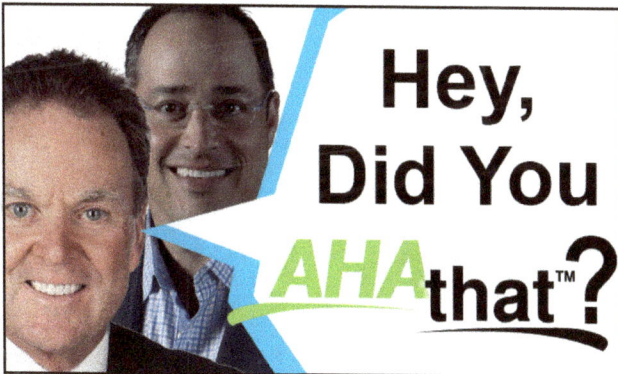

Please go directly to this book in AHAthat and share each AHAmessage socially at **http://aha.pub/SalesSuccessAHAs**.

www.ingramcontent.com/pod-product-compliance
Lightning Source LLC
Chambersburg PA
CBHW071208200326
41519CB00018B/5423